THE DECLINE OF SEX

To Sergeii, Olga, and Dmitri

THE DECLINE OF SEX

Fakes, phonies,
and America's shrinking libido

Pauly Jansen

It's not as if sex is new. The Pleasure Dome, Roman Imperial Orgies, and the Kama Sutra, all prove that people the world over have liked sex for at least 300 years, and perhaps even much longer.

.|.   .|.   .|.

Chapter 1: Inter-duction

The Fall of Sex might have presented a more abrupt and dramatic air as a title, but sex has not fallen. Instead it still lives, breathes, and moans in a diluted, confused state. Since about the early 1960s, this messy business of stroking, licking, poking, and squeezing has suffered from rude distractions on all sides. Physical barriers interfere with the direct touch of skin; pharmaceuticals alter our internal sensations; computers divert the craving gaze from the flesh to the flash of a screen; toys and machines fill in for absent partners. Even that one thing most deeply desired by humans, a long life, threatens our sex drive with extended boredom.

In just the past few years, we have succumbed to the ultimate of modern urges, to gadgetize everything including ourselves. No sooner did the pill liberate women from the risk of pregnancy than a raging cascade of implanted gizmos joined the scene. As sili-tits led to puffed up butts, and bleach blonde hair led to the dumbed-out Botox stare, our attention turned from having sex to having procedures that mimic jackass porn stars with the hottest shape. In only a few decades, adolescents with sweaty palms and swelling glands gave way to pharma-soothe-ical "coming on E". Naked togetherness was once a world changing leap for first time lovers, but now it seems to need chemical enhancement and maybe even a few reconstructive surgeries before breaking 15 years of age. We have given birth to cyber-sex, and are quickly becoming the sexual victims of our own techno-offspring. In other words, we fucked with technology, and now technology is fucking us right back.

(.) (.)   (.) (.)   (.) (.)

Chapter 2: The Lay of the Land

Ian Dury said that *Sex & Drugs & Rock & Roll* are all his brain and body need (...very good indeed). Dury played his music rough and ready but he also kept his lyrics nicey-nice with a touch of class, meekly suggesting that you grab a small slice of the cake of liberty. *Wake Up and Make Love With Me* seems to be as much a gentle request for sex as a hint that he just might go ahead with it if you kept on sleeping (1977 the album *New Boots and Panties!!*). Just a year later, *Hit Me With Your Rhythm Stick* set a new high for complex and punchy Brit-rock, but the sexual innuendo remained as tame or as lame as ever. After all, the lyrics read more like a clever geography lesson than the penile reference that the titular 'rhythm stick' carries, rhyming Milan with Yucatan, or Borneo with Bordeaux. Bombay surely rhymes with Santa Fe, but where's the sex?

The Exploited might have brought creativity to grand new heights, but the job of pulling the pants down on sex in music hasn't even gotten past the zipper yet. Here is a taste. *Sex and Violence* stands as the first song in history that uses its own title as the entire lyrics (1981 album *Punks Not Dead*.) It goes something like this, so see if you can manage to follow along...

> sex and violence,
> sex and violence,
> sex,
> and violence,
> sex and violence, sex and violence...

It grinds on like this for over 5 minutes, beating its own head to a bloody anarchic pulp, repeating the same line about 56 times, first at a walking pace, but soon enough builds to a gasping, sweaty, mind-buzzing rage. This is true genius, but again, it's musical genius and not the breakout in sexual explicitness that we've been craving for thousands of years since Emperor Nero fiddled and diddled. The song only offers a petty, straightforward slogan no riskier than the typical 1930s jazz duets that sang about sliding your long, lean, juicy hot dog into my big warm roll. Listen to some Butterbeans and Susie, they'll make you groan.

While musicians slowly advanced the sexual content of their lyrics, a few rural towns also edged their way into the risqué name game. Canada's most easterly province, Newfoundland, endorses Dury's ready-to-go position, and, in true exhibitionist spirit, splashes its feist on highway signs from coast to coast. Town names like Dildo and Conception Bay (yes, really) attest to the region as having the highest sex rate in the country (by the way, Dildo's town motto is reported to be Oh-I've-Never-Thought-of-That). Come-By-Chance sure as hell didn't just come by chance (I heard a rumor that the original name "Premature-Ejaculation" was rejected after a squeaky tight vote at the municipal council). Blow-Me-Down is miles away from Hearts Content, although the name suggests that it could be a suburb. Woody Point? Its residents stand erect and purple faced, with bulging pride. No other province compares, although others do make feeble hearted attempts. Balls Falls Ontario comes in at an ass kissing second best, while the road sign leading into Climax Saskatchewan invites you to 'come again'. Literally.

But I digress. All this juvenile grade horniness only shows the urge for sex lives strong in one isolated zone at the edge of the ocean. Let's jiggle our collective ass back into the cultural mainstream to see the full-throated future of sexy.

Frank Zappa's *Dinah-Moe-Humm* came up quickly from behind and handcuffed America into musical submission (1973 album *Over-nite Sensation*). Orgasm was the whole point, and Dinah dared you to give her one if you were man enough to do it. She even bet you a $40 bill that you couldn't. You weasely wiener.

Dinah-Moe-Humm took a direct shot at prudes in 1973, but it would take 6 more years for *Bobby Brown* to give us a sweet first taste of true 'modern love' (with apologies to David Bowie). Bobby goes to an Ivy League school and imagines himself as the American Dream, a smooth, slick dick that no chick can resist. After contemplating raping a classmate who helps him with his homework, the narcissistic Bobby insults all college girls, and feminism in general, and inadvertently hooks up with a lesbian named Freddie who teaches him a few things about sex toys and bad lube. His will and his balls broken, he placidly converts to homosexuality, and learns to enjoy the tower of power which, of course, rhymes with golden showers. Some people see Dinah and Bobby as innocuous fun, but Zappa was rarely innocuous. This was an early reading of the budding new sexual landscape of gadgets and enhancement, with lyrics of some considerable insinuation and bite.

Frank also took an early poke at new-tech like micro-derm abrasion, referring to it as sandblasting your ghastly zits.

Rockers and Punks were not alone in the musical hormone zone. The legendary Funk-a-teer Bootsy Collins said right out loud that Funk was created in a nasty place, somewhere between a butt-hole and a pee-hole, and that, "... it was gooood and it was nasty, nothin' is good unless you play with it, and we played with, it with both hands." Social progress seemed imminent at long last, but no matter how hard these musical warriors fought this noble fight, the forces of decline proved to be indomitable.

It took Nancy Reagan and a stunned posse of conservative fogies a few short years to catch up with the brave new wave of explicitness, replying with the pathetic "Just Say No" campaign. This was the best advice that republicans could devise to help the nation's kids deal with the mounting peer pressure surrounding sex and drugs (they could have bitten back with a giant 'fuck you', but somehow chose to demur). Although drugs were named as the campaign's target, sex avoidance also lay clearly within the message. It's just that this tight-right bunch could only feel at ease being explicit about getting high, not about getting off.

They had a long tradition of prohibiting drugs from cocaine, heroin and weed to alcohol, whereas they didn't have the first idea of how to address the sex that instilled a vile fear and loathing in the faithful. In the end, the so-called moral majority even avoided *talking* about avoiding sex but it was plain to see that the fight was on to slow the love train.

The running shoe maker Nike seems to have snatched at the chance to poke Nancy in the eye and redirect the conversation along sexual lines with a clever little touch, adopting "Just Do It" as their corporate tagline. (*Nike Poked Nancy* might make a cute movie title one day.) A legendary spoofy T-shirt later replied "Just Did It", which might have spawned the creepy new father-daughter virgin movement. What a mess, but more on that later.

.I.   .I.   .I.

Chapter 3: Chairman of the Bored

Remember George Carlin's Pills:
Baby-Maybe and Preg-Not

What is the perfect pair? Having babies without sex and having sex without babies. Talk about upside down. Techno-sex has undone nature from both ends. *In-vitro* fertilization is nothing more than outsourced copulation without any copulation at all. Instead of stroking and poking, your doctor reaches in to grab the little goodies and then mixes them up in a lab dish.

What's next? Hands-free masturbation? We were almost there in the 90s with vibrating movie seats, smell-surround, and wrap-around goggles, but virtual reality has virtually died since the turn of the century. Maybe it will make a true comeback when web pornographers merge with computer makers and figure out how to 'put you in the picture'. Call 310-Dildo ?

Medical hi-tech works as well for preventing babies as it does for making babies. Modern contraception comes in a virtual war-chest of anti-baby technology including pharma-chemicals, mechanical gadgets, synthetic latex, and precision surgery. In just a few decades, reproductive science has toppled the entire course of contraceptive history and changed the nature of the sex act. Freer and more relaxed? Of course. But you also might have thought that all of this loosening up would usher in a gusher of sex, maybe even enough to overwhelm the legions of moralizers, abstainers, born-again virgins (I call these the Un-fucked) and religios who never stop trying to stop you from having a good time. You might have thought wrong, cuz all the perfect techno-contraptions in the world haven't touched the main drag of sexual decline, boredom.

As the old line goes, "...if you're gonna screw me, please use lube or buy me dinner first". In other words, I'd prefer that you didn't bone me dry, but rather that you ease it in a bit more gently. Now, dinner has always been used to grease the path toward a sexual encounter. Eating engages four out of the five main senses as we gaze at the gorgeous plate, smell the arousing aromas, feel the velvety and crispy textures, and taste the succulent flavors. No wonder we slide into sex more easily when our appetite has been primed by food. After all, the mouth is every bit as much a sex organ as the Va-j-j; the eyes appreciate an oozing cream pie as much as our glistening loins.

But speaking of sliding into sex, America shows as much division on this topic as on politics or religion. Some middle-aged fogies, especially republicans, have been heard to complain that their wives are actually too wet for them to enjoy. If that's as clever as they can get, then we can only suspect that these guys will actively seek out and use almost any excuse not to have sex. This entirely weird angle on sex avoidance exposes yet another twist in the psyched-out roots of the decline of sex.

On the other hand, the lubrication industry comes to the rescue when we can't slide so easily on our own. Millions of women have convinced themselves that they need an additive because they don't produce as much natural juice as they did at a younger age. Or maybe it's really because boredom begins to set in after a long marriage? Who knows, but technology is always the willing partner, ready to sell you whatever you think you might need. Sure, a nice big spurt of Astro-glide gives you a hole new sensation, but it's also yet another sign of the decline, another sign of tech-no-sex, of enhancement instead of enchantment.

Enhancement now parades as variety. You can have a thick bumpy one, a jiggly transparent green one, some goop with a minty taste, or maybe a sparky, scratchy electric gizmo for your poop-chute. All of this enhanced variety supposedly improves the experience. A big purple dildo enhances the touch, especially when your man is away. But, if he's the one using it on you, the device adds one degree of separation. Sure it's a change, but why stop there? Big plastic tits also enhance the look, but hey babe, it just ain't you. If you think that your big new puffy sili-tits really improve you, then why don't you wear a Jessica Simpson mask for me too? You'd be a hole lot prettier and I could call you Daisy, you know, just for a bit more variety. Meantime, I'll get a Brad Pitt facelift and maybe some implants for my little pecs. Are you hot for me now?

So, does the rising use of gizmos and gadgets mirror the decline of sex? Is sex actually in decline? Here is yet another piece of compelling evidence. A report from the UK's Daily Mail suggests that longer relationships produce more boredom, at least for women. The super hot action starts with the most scintillating headline ever to be given to an article on sex... "How a woman's sex drive declines over time - and a man's stays as strong as ever". I bet you're just dying to see how this one goes.

The original report comes from the Journal of Sex & Marital Therapy, yes, another fireball of a name. Just keep in mind that the research was done in Canada, a country somewhere in the north that's said to be a mere tenth the size of America. Imagine. That implies that America's problem with sex is ten times larger. This pipsqueak of a study was done by a student at the University of Guelph, an institution once known as "Cow College", and that's a fact, Jack. One might wonder, in passing, exactly what the hell a *Guelph* is, or maybe not. Let's just move along with the findings.

The study's 170 subjects were all undergrads from U of Guelph and their relationships ranged from 1 month to 9 years in length, which probably means that they are not very old. In brief, the report shows an unsurprising steady fall in women's sexual desire with each passing month of the relationship, as opposed to the shocking news that the men's desire level stayed up. You can just imagine how the results would go if they studied couples with 30 or 40 year relationships.

One Daily Mail reader posted a comment saying that it only proves women get progressively more bored of being with the same man. That man gets fatter and fatter, which is more and more of a turn off for the woman. That's no surprise, but then neither is the view from the men's side, that women gain many pounds of their own while the "I do" at the altar turns into "I don't" for the B-J. The strange part here may be that the men did not report a decline in sexual interest, although the author thinks this might be because men don't accurately report their feelings. In other words, there may be some plain old lying from the testosterone-charged guy faction. After all the shit-slinging, accusations, name calling, and denials, all we're left with is the bare-assed fact that people sexually tire of each other as they spend more time together.

So once again, in the end, all of the sex toys, potions, and custom body jobs just look like diversions or cover-ups for boredom. This is the boredom of long-in-the-tooth marriages, or, for all you hot busy singles, maybe even the boredom of going through the same old dating-mating routines too many times with too many partners. Even so, the e-sex industry keeps on spurting out new ways to avoid the dripping mess of real sex... HD photos; streaming porn videos; sexting. Even the kids now convince themselves that it's medically safer to have e-sex than to physically see each other. OK, here's a pop quiz... what's the next mobile device? Maybe an i-Guy? Or an i-Snatch? I invite you to look up Roxxxy and Rocky. But for now, it's touch-screens only, please... stay dry, use a gadget! Maybe I'll just get high with the all new i-Pot.

(.) (.)   (.) (.)   (.) (.)

Chapter 4: Aging Nuts

As you approach the more serious stages of aging, your eyes deteriorate in synch with your partner's looks. That's one of the few times that nature will ever do you a favor of any kind. Aside from that magnanimous gift, aging is all crap. Sometimes in your pants. You get fat and can't find your junk. If you do manage to find it, half the time it doesn't work worth a shit. If it does happen to work at all, it's more than likely that your partner won't be interested because they are getting old and clapped out too. If and when they do get a little spark of interest, you will have forgotten what the fuck you were there to do in the first place. And finally (yes, Virginia, it gets even worse), if you get around to doing the messy little deed, your new extended lifespan pretty much guarantees that one or both of you will get thoroughly bored of the whole thing before you can even finish it. After 53 years of marriage, you have been over the same territory so many times that you could practically do it in your sleep. So that's exactly what you do. Love you too. Good night.

All of that heartbreaking misery comes to you on account of the technology that keeps you healthy longer, or saves your life from extreme situations that would have killed someone like you just a few decades ago. Medicine, diagnostic prevention, occupational therapy, prosthetics, implants, and other gizmos all conspire to lengthen your life and vastly raise the chance that you will be sexless for a long time. Viagra? Sounds good as long as you enjoy a patented, chemically induced erection that comes along with the chance of nausea and low blood pressure. Is that not such a big deal, old man? Then you might discover what fetishers have known for centuries. They all wear off, and most guys need to find a new fetish each time the last one ceases to stimulate him. Same goes for psychotherapy, the 20th century way to adjust your mind to make you desire just the right amount of sex. For too little sex there is marriage counseling; for too much sex you can get addiction counseling (so 1984-ish). But just as patients become tolerant to drugs, talk therapy wears off. Most induced arousal methods might work for about 2 years before fading, so if you want to use the chemical route anyway, then go crazy!

As recently as the 1950s, people died young enough that sex was still a part of their lives. They got killed in industrial accidents, by flu epidemics, or by sudden heart attacks. Most of that was solved by the lifesaving miracle of the 911 emergency telephone system and modern hospitals. Tech strikes again, right in the nuts.

.l.   .l.   .l.

Chapter 5: Wash Your Ass

Redd Foxx said that if you really love your partner, you have got to wash your ass. Not your whole ass, but your ass-hooooole.

Now, Foxx was a master seducer and he knew that clean means that you respect your mate, but also that you don't turn them off with your all-natural down low stank. This is a uniquely human concern. Most other animals deliberately and doggedly seek the stank. They relish the raunch. They savor the stench.

A dog's ass is at just the same level as another dog's nose. Same with chimps. Many Darwinian scientists think that humans evolved to walk on two feet because it's just cleaner to keep your nose out of another person's ass. But even though evolution took care of separating the sniffer from the shitter, we keep bringing new scent oriented technology into the bathroom so as to reduce the chance of turning off the other sex. The irony is that we're virtually paranoid about being sexually attractive, even while we keep inventing new ways of avoiding sex.

(.) (.)　　(.) (.)　　(.) (.)

Chapter 6: Puppy Love

The ancient Greeks were famed for their love of lamb. Not as a dinner course, of course, but another-course altogether. They were said to, ahem, love their lambs. In a similar vein, the ancient Kazakhs were rumored by some to love their camels, a charge made all the more plausible if the recent Borat films have any credibility. The story does not seem to apply to America today, but a strange or even creepy parallel does crop up. As the country's sex rate declines, the pet ownership rate rises.

No one is saying that Americans have replaced romantic love with a panting lust after their dogs, but there is no denying the simultaneous trends of less sex and more pets. As life spans and relationships grow ever longer, people subconsciously seek distractions from their spouse. "The kids are all gone, so why don't we get a dog? That would be so nice, honey." "Of course it would dear, I could play with a puppy instead of listening to you drone on about your bad knees."

Some psychiatrists call this sublimation, although the details are a bit skewed in this case. In the usual setting, the subject has a pent up sexual energy but doesn't have enough of an outlet. This patient is undersexed but instead of forcing himself on an unwilling or difficult partner, he channels his sexual desire toward another activity such as art or literature. The sexual drive is transformed from what used to be seen as a base, primal urge into a higher or more sublime one, hence the word sublimation.

Now in the modern age of overextended relationships, the sexual desire does not completely disappear, but it does get pushed aside. And in being pushed aside, that energy remains available to focus on similar objects. Like what? Like dogs. It's not sex, but the similarity should be obvious. People love petting and stroking their dogs. Many people admit that they love the smell of a clean dog. Then there is all the licking and cuddling and grooming and ooohing and aawing. This is puppy love and it is definitely an outlet that reduces the amount of real sex. Watch for this to take hold and spread as younger generations of families adopt dogs at an earlier age. Puppies especially act as a non-sexual distraction to blossoming adolescents whose raging hormones can otherwise only be dealt with by real sex or self-service. As the average family size shrinks toward one child, the younger sibling will more and more often be a dog that absorbs household's excess the time, attention and affection. It's not bestiality, but I'm just saying.

(.) (.)   (.) (.)   (.) (.)

Chapter 7: Back to the Future

Germis: sweet or odorless shaven vulva

The very same parents who be-moan the pube-ification of pre-teen youth are those who try the hardest to return to a pre-pube look. They may not recognize it because they mostly use the simplest technology, but it is technology nonetheless. Scissors, electric razors, wax, sugar and such.

Women have now completed the shaving cycle that started with armpits and lower legs. Laser takes care of stray 'stache hairs while the Brazilians look after the strays at the back door. And now that Sinbad O'Connor has faded from pop music we can breathe a collective sigh of relief that women chose a slick snapper over a chrome dome. An entire Western culture hopes that a clean shaven female head never makes a comeback.

The *germis* first came out in the late 70s as some well established porn rags like Hustler competed with the earliest raunch videos to show more feminine skin than previously thought possible. The lips came out of hiding. When the boys followed, they all said that it made their meat look longer, and it really did, so of course the look was here to stay. Who could resist?

By the time your mom took up the clippers, dad told himself that it must be cleaner and it must smell better, and that was why he liked it. By the time your dad heard about man-scaping, mom yearned for that little bit more, that extra heft her last boyfriend had before she married, and this would be a clean way to get it. It's not how big it is, it's all about how big you *think* it is. So the moment of truth is here, and the truth is that the "tidy" look of shaving, whatever else it might be, is also the look of pre-puberty.

The obsession with youth that advertisers express as kids in lingerie and eyeliner has deeply penetrated the American adult psyche, even to the point where they are doing it to themselves by depilating their sex organs. The middle aged and the elderly looked down and found the easiest way to look like a kid again. Exactly like a kid. A bit of low-tech grooming and viola!, don't I look young? Growing up used to mean wanting to look like an adult, but now it means wanting to look like a baby (watch for breast and penis reductions coming soon at a sex-tech-clinic near you). Shaving, plucking, laser, waxing, bleaching, acid-cremes... the kids are doing it too, being all unhip to flash bush, but the cutest bit has to be that they just unwittingly copied the porn stars who were copying them.

And baldness? It's nearly an exploding fad as guys of all ages shave and shine their cranium to a high luster at the first sign of hair loss. It takes the look right back to infancy. The look of old age used to be a receding hairline, but now the look of old age is the same as the look that old uncle Hank sported as he squirted out of the love canal 57 years ago. The circle of life takes on a whole new meaning. Meantime, anyone willing to talk to you will confirm that anti-hair enhances the sexual stimulus. True, but it also psyches everyone out with another dozen salon procedures to carry on in the hope of keeping the fire burning through ever longer decades of monogamous monotony.

I now have embedded in my mind the horrifying picture of granny with a clean-shaven thingy, tight skin, glossy sunglasses, and long neon green toenails, smooth platinum hair flowing down as gramps grins at her through his gleaming Hollywood-white smile. Barf out.

(.) (.)   (.) (.)   (.) (.)

Chapter 8: Pure Balls

America is famous for its split personality. It's the world's biggest spender in the war against drugs and the world's biggest drug consumer. It's simultaneously the land of puritans and the world's biggest producer of porn. Now it's also the sexiest country and the one trying hardest to abstain. How hard? Well, millions of Americans are actually trying to eliminate the sexual urge altogether. This is the intentional, deliberate decline of sex. As strange as it might sound, one man contributing to the decline goes by the name of Father John A. Hardon. It's true. You really should look it up. Father Hardon wants you to completely avoid sex unless you are married. Be a virgin, stay a virgin. Normally, I would not pay much attention to priests, but I've never heard of a talking Hardon. So when a Hardon speaks, I just can't help but prick up my ears to hear what he has to say. Sadly, we end up disappointed by our newly found Hardon because he brings nothing new to the table. His limp message turns out to be little more than the usual biblical pronouncements on chastity. Let's move on to some other players in the Virginity Industry.

Meet the purity dads. Here is a group of supposedly modern fathers building moral links with the woman haters among the hyperorthodox jews and the taliban all at the same time. Whether you own your daughters, dictate to your wife, or interfere with schoolgirls, the focus is on less sex and the only difference is in degree.

Purity dads devote a lot of time and energy to preventing their daughters from having sex. Starting at about 8 years of age, these little girls watch daddy take control and take ownership. They eventually give up and give in, and pledge their virginity to father. In return, father pledges to maintain *authority* over her 'purity'. How much creepier could it possibly get than to own your child's vagina? Maybe the virginity movement has designed this somewhat incestuous creep factor into their scheme as an extra assurance against the joy of sex. After all, associating sex with father from an early age creates a gross-out that will likely never quit.

These creepy fathers take their daughters to so-called Purity Balls, sometimes calling the evening a date, where a public display of dancing and affection allegedly substitutes for a young woman's dry, sexless years. They could have called them Proms, but no, for some reason they call them

Balls. One might have thought that they would avoid letting their daughters near any "balls" at all, much less the balls of their fathers. One thing usually remains true though; more father in a young woman's psyche leads to less sex. Mission accomplished, at least sometimes. This kind of plot has also been known to occasionally backfire, such as when Sweetness realizes that she's been duped and firmly decides to go on a fuck-fest in retaliation.

Chapter 9: Presidential Sweet

The founding fathers were a hot and bothered bunch. They yearned for a break from uptight Mother Britain, not only over high taxes, but over high religion and the reeking pretense of high morals. The Declaration of Independence dispenses with all of the old school god-talk and instead decrees that America stands for life, liberty, and the pursuit of happiness. As leader of this horny gang, Thomas Jefferson showed us that a statesman and scholar could also be a wine lover and a high-grade womanizer (perfectly rounded if you ask me). So this proves that the so-called 'pursuit of happiness' was a thinly veiled code inviting a lustful debauchery into the birth of a new free society. It was, in fact, an open invitation for a new kind of freedom, the likes of which has never been seen, for women to take up the "pursuit of a penis".

So what happened? Jefferson's plan worked for a while and he had his way more times than he could count. The country bloomed as family size increased, spreading a torrent of fertile liberty across the west before the civil war put a sudden end to a century of fun. A stern new wave squashed the American libido and spawned generations of new puritans seeking solace in the church. The coming decades of dry and crusty religious moralizing turned the land of freedom into the home of the grave. Church and state were officially separated, but by now Jesus had somehow become a wholly owned subsidiary of US industry. Henry Ford eventually sent his own Social Department to spy on his assembly workers in their homes, pretending to be father-priest of private morals and prohibiting booze. Jesus famously said "drink this wine", but Henry said "don't you dare". The bible said "go forth and multiply" but early evangelists said "keep it in your pants".

A long roster of grandfather-ish presidents reinforced this emotional repression with a sober and flabby look. Did the highest office ever host a hot papa? Woodrow Wilson? Calvin Coolidge? Herbert Hoover? What's up with all the presidential alliteration? What about Harry Truman or Ike? Nope. It wasn't until JFK took the White House that sex regained its position on top of America's Most Wanted list. The great decline of sex in America seemed, for just one brief shining moment, to have come to an end, an end brought about almost singlehandedly by the president who very publically came a lot. Then the hope of a sexual revival was dashed, as if sex itself was assassinated.

America suffered with ugly presidents for most of its history, so what's different now? Why would presidential sex appeal start to matter at all in the 60s? In a word, the collapse of a dream. JFK spawned a splendid new psyche in the American female, chance to fantasize about great power. His gorgeous and charming First Lady became the first lady worthy of emulation, and that's exactly what women did. They dressed how Jackie dressed, they copied her gentle manner, but most of all they imagined nuzzling up to the first truly hot president in a lifetime. Here was a man who played nuclear roulette with the Russians at lunch time, and cavorted with Marilyn in the evening. He gave magnificent speeches about duty and honor, then dallied at embassy parties all night long. Power may be sexy, but sexy power is something else altogether.

After a couple of years in office, American women had fixed their gaze on JFK, and fleeting glimpses of their dear leader popped into their romantic daydreams many times each day. The president became virtually synonymous with their sexual urges. The assassination shook the entire countries in so many ways that it almost seems impossible to reconcile. And the effects of an onslaught of old-man presidents has yet to even be recognized.

A grim lineup of grump, frump, and chump replaced the young and debonair Kennedy. Liberal, conservative, no matter, just look at these dour fellas, these sour pusses. Virtual copies of each other, from Johnson to Nixon to Ford, from Carter to Reagan to GHW Bush, and not a whiff of sex appeal. You could easily excuse someone for falling under the paranoid delusion of an anti-sex conspiracy hell bent on keeping attractive men out of the nation's highest office.

America needs a hot new president. Not Obama the Grey, and not Sarah "Pant-Suit" Palin. I'm thinking all natural, straight talking, and built. Someone who just oozes with sex appeal, and who isn't married to Hillary. Maybe a woman who cares more about human fulfillment than about taxes or Texas. Government should encourage a return to the raging free love of the 1960s, and maybe even ban a few so-called sexual enhancement surgeries. It won't be easy but the results might be more fun than stressing out over a few wrinkles. We could recruit some Libido Ambassadors to staff and spark up our hugely dismal government agencies. This is very nearly a national emergency, so FEMA sex officers should not be out of the question. Those who are still in the right weight class to be able to perform the sexual act may need to be conscripted, much like other state mandated duties in some countries, to perform it with those who are too bored to carry it out for themselves or with each other. President Obama has made a major anti-conservative move by proposing his high science Brain Initiative supported by billions in future funding. Maybe he'll wise up to the fact that a similar fund could unravel the American the libido and switch it back on, to everybody's glee.

NOTES

Index

F

fear and loathing, 8
FEMA, 39
fetish, 18
flash bush, 29
Frank Zappa, 6
fuck you, 7

G

gadgetize, 2
George Carlin, 9
Germis, 27
gizmos, 2, 12, 18
goop. *See* lube
granny, 29
gusher, 10

H

Hardon, 31
Hit Me With Your Rhythm Stick, 3
homosexuality, 6
Hustler. *See* porn rag

I

Ian Dury, 3, 5
implants, 18
induced arousal, 18
In-vitro, 9
i-Snatch, 15

J

jackass, 2
Jackie, 37

W